KT-488-462

10/23

5QP

my first book of
questions and answers

ships and
submarines

James Pickering

p

This is a Parragon Book
First published in 2002

Parragon
Queen Street House
4 Queen Street
Bath BA1 1HE, UK

Produced by

David West ᚛ Children's Books
7 Princeton Court
55 Felsham Road
Putney
London SW15 1AZ

British Library Cataloguing-in-Publication Data

A catalogue record for this book is available from
the British Library.

ISBN 0-75258-457-X

Printed in China

Designers
Axis Design, Aarti Parmar, Rob Shone,
Fiona Thorne

Illustrators
Mike Lacey, Geoff Pleasance (SGA)

Cartoonist
Peter Wilks (SGA)

Editor
Ross McLaughness

CONTENTS

4 What were the first boats made of?

4 Who put the first sails on boats?

5 Who invented rudders?

6 Who first sailed around the world?

6 How did Columbus reach America?

7 What is a sextant?

8 Why did triremes have rams?

8 Which warships carried gold?

9 What is a flagship?

10 Which roads are made of water?

10 Which taxis travel on water?

11 What is a narrowboat?

12 When were submarines invented?

12 What was a diving barrel?

13 When was a submarine first used in battle?

14 Which boat first ran on steam?

14 Who crossed the Atlantic by steam?

15 Which steam boats have paddles?

16 What was an ironclad warship?

16 Can ships carry planes?

17 Who hunted in 'wolf packs'?

18 What is a nuclear submarine?

18 Which ships use nuclear power?

19 What is a Typhoon?

20 What is a container ship?

20 What is a ro-ro?

21 Which are the largest ships?

22 What are the fastest sailing boats?

22 How fast can boats go?

23 Which boat is a cat?

24 Who skis on the water?

24 Who sails on a board?

25 Which boats have handlebars?

26 How do sailors know where they are?

26 How do fishing boats find their catch?

27 How do ships see in fog?

28 What are micro-subs?

28 What are Alvin and Jason Junior?

29 Which sub can dive the deepest?

30 What travels on a cushion of air?

31 Which boats have wings?

31 Which ship is invisible?

32 Index

What were the first boats made of?

The first sailors rowed in hollowed out tree trunks and coracles. A coracle is made out of bendy sticks covered in an animal skin.

Coracle

Ancient Egyptian sailing boats

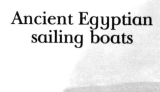

Who put the first sails on boats?

The Ancient Egyptians first put sails on boats about 5,000 years ago. They realised that wind-power would make their sailing boats much faster than rowing boats.

Chinese junk

❓ Who invented rudders?

A rudder is a flap at the back of a boat, which is used for steering. The Chinese first put rudders on wooden boats called junks over 1,000 years ago. Junks are still sailed in China today.

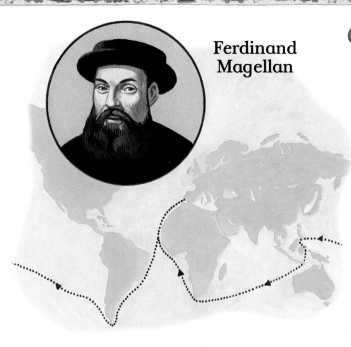

Ferdinand Magellan

❓ Who first sailed around the world?

Ferdinand Magellan commanded the first round the world trip. He died during the voyage, but one of his ships returned home. Starting in 1519, the journey took nearly three years.

❓ How did Columbus reach America?

In 1492, Christopher Columbus made a voyage across the Atlantic Ocean with three sailing ships, Santa Maria, Pinta and Niña. He discovered America by accident – he was trying to sail to Japan on the other side of the world!

? What is a sextant?

A sextant is an instrument which helped early sailors find their way. They used it to take measurements of the Sun and stars to work out where they were and if they were on course.

Sailor using a sextant

Columbus first used a compass.

FALSE. Chinese sailors were already using compasses to find their way about 400 years before Columbus made his voyage to America.

Hernan Cortes discovered the potato.

FALSE. Sir Walter Raleigh first discovered potatoes. Cortes made an even better discovery – chocolate!

❓ Why did triremes have rams?

Ancient Greek battleships called triremes had huge battering rams on their bows. If they came across an enemy ship, they could sink it by punching a hole in its side with the ram!

Trireme

❓ Which warships carried gold?

Galleons were large trading and fighting ships, which crossed the Atlantic Ocean between Europe and America. They had plenty of room to carry lots of precious gold back home.

Admiral Nelson's flagship – HMS Victory

? What is a flagship?

The admiral is the most important person in the navy. In the old days, he used to sail in the flagship, which was usually the biggest and best looking of all the ships in the fleet.

TRUE OR FALSE?

The Mary Rose had so many guns it sank.

TRUE. The Mary Rose was King Henry the Eighth's flagship. It sank because of all the heavy guns it was carrying on board.

Pirates sailed under the skull and crossbones.

TRUE. Some pirates had a frightening skull and crossbones on their flag. Others had a plain black flag.

Which roads are made of water?

Canals are man-made 'water roads'. They're used by barges, which carry goods through the countryside. The first canals were built to provide quick and safe travel, before cars and trains were invented.

Canal

Which taxis travel on water?

The city of Venice in Italy has no roads for cars. Instead, the streets are filled with water, and everyone travels around the city in boats. 'Taxi-boats' in Venice are called 'gondolas'.

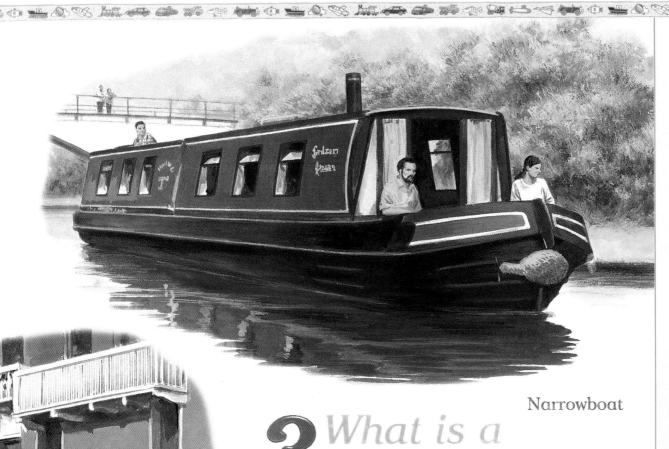

Narrowboat

Canal boats were pulled by horses.

TRUE. Early canal boats didn't have engines. Horses on the bank used to pull them instead.

Large ships can't use canals.

FALSE. The Panama Canal in Central America is very wide, and is used by enormous ships every day.

❓ What is a narrowboat?

Canals aren't just used for work – some people take holidays on them too. A narrowboat is like a floating home, complete with a kitchen, beds, bathroom, and sometimes even a television!

When were submarines invented?

The first submarine was built in 1620 by Cornelius Drebbel. Engines had not been invented, so the submarine had oars like a rowing boat. The crew breathed through a tube to the surface.

Drebbel's submarine

Diving barrel

What was a diving barrel?

A diving barrel was an early type of diving suit, invented in 1721. Divers could see underwater through a glass peephole. They spent more time rising to the surface to breathe than swimming!

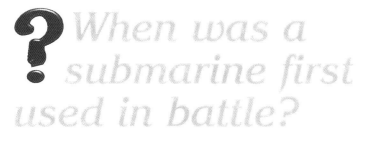

? When was a submarine first used in battle?

When America and Britain were at war in 1776, the Americans tried to blow up a British ship, using a tiny submarine called Turtle. Their plan didn't work. One person sat inside Turtle, turning its propeller by hand.

Turtle

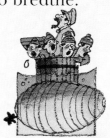

Which boat first ran on steam?

Pyroscaphe was built in 1783, and had two steam-powered paddle wheels. Its engines were so noisy that they shook the boat to bits after only 15 minutes!

Pyroscaphe

Who crossed the Atlantic by steam?

Savannah used steam and sail power to cross the Atlantic Ocean in 1819. Sirius made the journey on steam power alone in 1838. The crew ran out of fuel, and had to burn the furniture to keep the engine going!

Savannah

? *Which steam boats have paddles?*

Most steam boats used paddles to push them through the water before propellers were invented. Paddles work very well in shallow water where propellers would get stuck in mud or weeds.

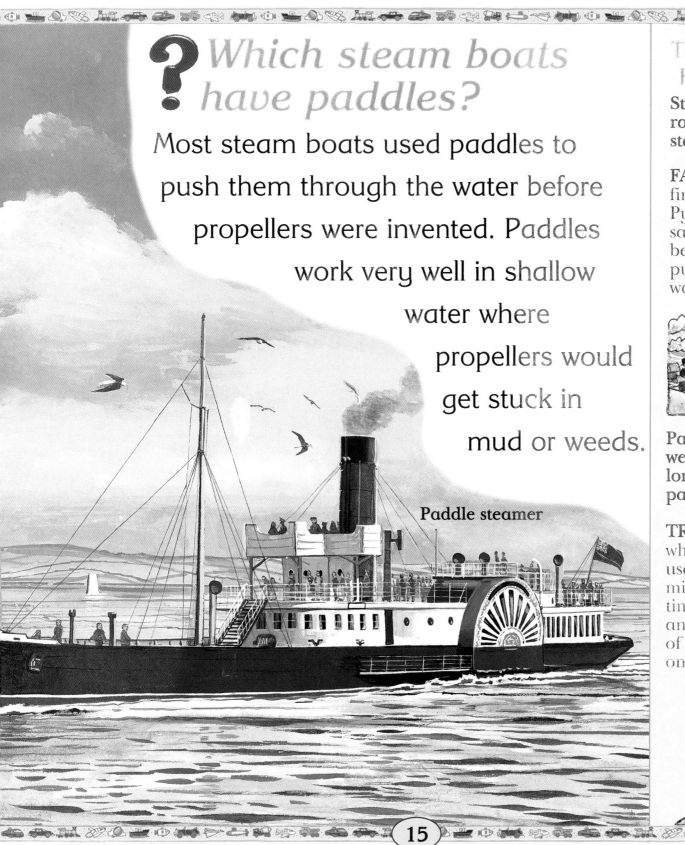

Paddle steamer

What was an ironclad warship?

Ironclads were ships which were armoured with iron. The first ironclads to meet in battle were Monitor and Merrimack, during the American Civil War in 1862. The ships were equally matched – neither of them won the battle.

Aircraft carrier

Merrimack

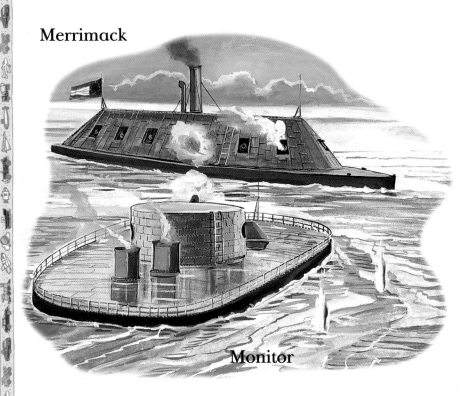

Monitor

Can ships carry planes?

Special navy ships called aircraft carriers look like floating airports. The deck is a long runway, where jet planes can take off and land at sea, instead of flying all the way back to land.

? Who hunted in 'wolf packs'?

German submarines called U-boats used to creep up in large groups and attack other ships. People thought the groups of U-boats looked like packs of wolves on a hunt, and therefore nicknamed them 'wolf packs'.

U-boat

TRUE OR FALSE?

Some planes are launched by catapult.

TRUE. Aeroplanes need plenty of speed to take off from an aircraft carrier. Special catapults help to shoot them off the runway.

Cars can't float.

FALSE. The German army built a car, which could float through rivers. No one ever dared to sail it at sea!

? What is a nuclear submarine?

In the old days, submarines ran on diesel and electric power. They had to come up to the surface quite often to recharge their batteries. Modern nuclear-powered submarines don't need to do this, and can stay underwater for months on end.

Nuclear submarine

? Which ships use nuclear power?

Aircraft carriers and icebreakers are nuclear-powered. They can stay at sea for a very long time without having to refuel, just like nuclear submarines. Icebreakers are very strong ships, which cut through frozen seas, to make a path for other ships.

What is a Typhoon?

Typhoon

Russian Typhoons are the biggest and fastest submarines in the world. At 170 m, the Typhoon is as long as one and a half football pitches.

Icebreaker

Subs travel at the bottom of the ocean.

FALSE. The Pacific Ocean is nearly 11,000 m deep, but the deepest a submarine can dive is only about 700 m.

Subs carry their own air.

TRUE. Submarines carry tanks of air, just like scuba divers, so that the crew can breathe when they're underwater.

❓ What is a container ship?

Container ships carry cargo in metal boxes called containers. Cranes load the containers, which are taken away by truck at the end of the journey.

Container ship

❓ What is a ro-ro?

Ro-ro is short for 'roll on, roll off'. Ro-ro ferries carry cars, trucks and other vehicles, which drive up a gangplank on to the ferry at the start of the journey. They drive straight off again at the

Ro-ro ferry

? *Which are the largest ships?*

Oil tankers are the largest ships in the world. The world's biggest oil tanker weighs ten times more than the biggest ever car ferry.

Oil tanker

TRUE OR FALSE?

Oil tankers cannot stop in a hurry.

TRUE. Tankers are so big that they carry on for several kilometres before they can turn around or stop.

You can take a holiday on board a ship.

TRUE. Ocean liners are massive floating hotels. There are restaurants on board, as well as cinemas, nightclubs, and swimming pools!

Yacht

❓ What are the fastest sailing boats?

Modern yachts are very strong and fast. They use wind power, not an engine, and can be sailed for fun or in races. Skilled crews can even race their yachts all the

❓ How fast can boats go?

Powerboats are the fastest boats in the world. Some of them can travel at about 220 kph, as fast as an express train! It's a very bumpy ride, because they skim across the surface of the water and bounce off the waves.

Powerboat racing

? *Which boat is a cat?*

A catamaran, or cat for short, has two hulls below its deck. Cats are faster than yachts with only one hull.

Catamaran

TRUE OR FALSE?

Cargo ships are very slow.

FALSE. Inventors are trying to build a catamaran cargo ship, which would travel through the water as quickly as a speed boat.

Some boats have jet engines.

TRUE. The fastest boat ever was the jet-powered Spirit of Australia, which reached an amazing 511 kph!

Who skis on the water?

It's tricky, but great fun, to be towed on waterskis behind a speed boat. Expert skiers can even waterski barefoot without skis, and perform stunts.

Waterskiing

Who sails on a board?

A windsurf board is one of the smallest boats you can sail on. You stand on the board, holding on to the sail, turning it from side to side to steer. Some windsurfers can take off on their boards, and

Jetski

Windsurf board

❓ *Which boats have handlebars?*

Jetskis look like motorcycles whizzing across the water. Just as you would on a motorcycle, you speed up by twisting the handlebar, but instead of wheels, jetskis have water jets at the back, driven by a powerful motor.

How do sailors know where they are?

Four satellites in different parts of outer space send a radio signal to a ship at the same time. The signals take different amounts of time to reach the ship, and a computer compares them to work out where the ship is.

How do fishing boats find their catch?

Sonar computer

Fishing boats find fish with a system called sonar. This sends out high-pitched sounds into the water. If the sounds hit a school of fish, the echoes bounce back to the boat, and a computer works out where the fish are.

Radar screens

Ship's bridge
(control room)

❓ *How do ships see in fog?*

Ships see in fog with radar. A radio signal is sent out, and if it hits another boat or object, the signal bounces back and tells the ship where it is.

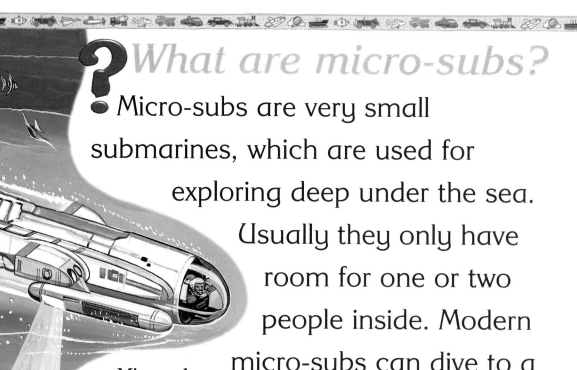

? What are micro-subs?

Micro-subs are very small submarines, which are used for exploring deep under the sea. Usually they only have room for one or two people inside. Modern micro-subs can dive to a

Micro-sub

? What are Alvin and Jason Junior?

Alvin is a micro-sub, which can carry three people. Jason Junior is a robot sub, which is operated from Alvin or from a ship on the surface. They explore shipwrecks on the seabed.

Alvin

? *Which sub can dive the deepest?*

An extra-strong micro-sub called Trieste managed to dive to nearly 11 km beneath the surface of the Pacific Ocean – the deepest dive ever!

Trieste

Micro-subs can dive deeper than submarines.

TRUE. Most submarines can only dive to about 450 m. The average micro-sub can dive about twice as deep.

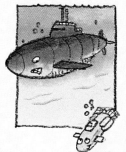

You can holiday in a submarine.

FALSE. Submarines are only used to patrol the seas during peace, and for combat during wartime.

? What travels on a cushion of air?

A hovercraft is not really a boat, because it doesn't travel through the water. Instead, it flies a few centimetres above the waves, on a cushion of air. Hovercraft can travel over land as well.

Hydrofoil

Hovercraft

Which boats have wings?

A hydrofoil has wings called foils on its underside, which stay underwater when it's not moving. But when the hydrofoil speeds up, its foils work like an aeroplane's wings, and lift the front of the hydrofoil into the air for high-speed travel.

Which ship is invisible?

The United States Navy's 'stealth' warship has a special shape and paint, which scatter enemy radar signals and make it very difficult to find.

'Stealth' warship

Index

aircraft carriers 16, 17, 18

Alvin 28

barges 10

canals 10, 11

catamaran 23

container ships 20

coracles 4

diving barrel 12

flagship 9

galleons 8

gondolas 10

hovercraft 30

hydrofoil 31

icebreakers 18

ironclads 16

Jason Junior 28

jetski 25

junks 5

Merrimack 16

micro-subs 28

Monitor 16

narrowboats 11

Niña 6

oil tankers 21

paddle steamer 15

Pinta 6

powerboats 22

Pyroscaphe 14

radar 27

ro-ro ferries 20

Santa Maria 6

satellites 26

Savannah 14

sextant 7

Sirius 14

sonar 26

'stealth' ship 31

steam boats 14, 15

submarines 12, 13, 18, 19, 28, 29

Trieste 29

triremes 8

Turtle 13

Typhoons 19

U-boats 17

waterskiing 24

windsurfing 24

yachts 22